THE FIVE DEADLY SHOULDS OF OFFICE POLITICS

OF OFFICE POLITICS

HOW THEY MANGLE YOUR CAREER (AND WHAT TO DO ABOUT THEM)

GRACE L. JUDSON

ISBN 13: 978-1523769223

ISBN 10: 152376922X

TABLE OF CONTENTS

Beware of Dragons 1
    What Are Politics? 2

Politics in the Office versus Politics Everywhere 7
    Shifting the Paradigm 9

How to Use This Book 11
    A Note on the Case Studies 11

First Dragon: I SHOULD be able to succeed without
participating in office politics 13
    POWER 13
    Two Ways the First Dragon Mangles Your Career 14
    Case Study 17

Second Dragon: I SHOULD get recognition for my work
without having to sell myself 19
    RESPONSIBILITY 20
    Two Ways the Second Dragon Mangles Your Career 20
    Case Study 22

Third Dragon: I SHOULD be able to trust my friends at work
to have my best interests at heart. 25
    TRUST 26

Two Ways the Third Dragon Mangles Your Career 26

Case Study 28

Fourth Dragon: It SHOULD be safe for me to tell the truth.31

TRUTH 32

Two Ways the Fourth Dragon Mangles Your Career............. 32

Case Study 35

Fifth Dragon: Senior management SHOULD always know
what they're doing. 37

COURAGE 37

Two Ways the Fifth Dragon Mangles Your Career 38

Case Study 41

Exercises and Worksheets 43

Introduction 43

The Fundamental Misconception 43

Power 47

A New Definition 47

POWER 47

In Action 49

Worksheet 50

Exercise: Step Into Your Power of Self 51

Responsibility 55

A New Definition 55

RESPONSIBILITY 55

In Action 56

Worksheet 57

Exercise: Acknowledge Your Excellence 59

Trust 63

A New Definition 63

TRUST 64

In Action 65

Worksheet 65

Exercise: Manage your Trust Foundation............................ 67

Truth 69

A New Definition.. 69

TRUTH.. 69

In Action 70

Worksheet 71

Exercise: Learn to See the Three Truths 72

Courage... 77

A New Definition.. 77

COURAGE... 77

Worksheet 79

Exercise: Practice Smart Courage....................................... 81

Afterword 85

About the Author 87

Praise for the Book.. 89

Praise for Grace.. 91

Beware of Dragons

Office politics has a bad reputation. Employees in corporations, academia, public service, nonprofits, science – anyone who works in any type of office – often feel as if they're fighting a continual battle: their values and integrity versus their desire for a successful career – and even their desire to simply get something done.

When the choice lies between "playing the game" in order to have a successful career OR remaining true to your sense of self and your values, then careers, values, personal pride, self-image, and even lives take a painful beating.

If you choose to participate in office politics despite your belief that it's despicable or dishonorable, you're handing your self-image over as a hostage.

On the other hand, if you choose not to participate in politics because you believe it's despicable or dishonorable, then you're handing your career over as a hostage.

Neither alternative works well.

Fortunately, there's a third option that requires no sacrifices, no hostages, and no battles. It exists in full harmony with your integrity and your success. It's not without risk (no option is risk-free), but it is free from the integrity-versus-success dilemma.

What Are Politics?

You have a definition of politics. It's one you've been living with for a while. In fact, though you might think it's been developing as your career developed, you've had a relationship with politics since you were an infant blowing bubbles at your parents.

Let me tell you – no, let me show you a new definition of politics.

Politics are part of every human interaction.

When my college political science professors told me that, I scoffed.

And yet, as I've come to realize and even appreciate, politics are happening all the time, especially in our closest relationships, and obviously in our workplaces.

**Politics are the *heart* and *soul*
of human interaction.**

How we manage this has a tremendous impact on how we feel, how we act, and how well we succeed.

Let me show you what I mean with these examples that are factual descriptions of real events that happened either to me or to my clients.

Your friend Bob sends you a terse email asking for a favor. It's *so* terse that you find yourself checking your job description to make sure it didn't suddenly morph into "Bob's minion." You're breathless. You're hurt. Then you're really pissed off.

But you choose to wait before you respond. Then, when you've calmed down and feel ready, you write an email that tells him and you that you still love him, though his wording made you sad. And the relationship is saved ... and actually deepened.

A storm was weathered, and it was weathered because you played *heartfelt* politics.

Your boss bites your head off because you commented to co-workers that a management emergency bumped your meeting from its scheduled conference room. You crawl back to your cubicle and wonder if you'll ever understand the rules of politics.

Then you decide to think about what's really going on instead of taking it personally. And you realize a few things.

- She's stressed because senior management as a group is tense about their decision for a corporate restructuring.
- That corporate restructuring has everyone looking over their shoulders worrying whether the next step is a company-wide layoff.
- And your comment – in a public hallway – was fuel for the layoff-rumor fire.

While her toothy response was her mistake, you see now that you'd have been better off simply smiling and mentioning that someone else needed the conference room.

This serves several beneficial purposes.

First, it's more merciful to those who might have overheard and gotten worried about job security.

Secondly, it's more honest. You have no real knowledge that there was a "management emergency" that bumped you from the conference room. It is, after all, senior management's prerogative to boost people out of conference rooms!

Thirdly, it's a wiser move for your career as well as your integrity.

In this case, you missed an opportunity to play empathetic politics.

The company president gives you responsibility for a major new project, a cross-departmental, mission-critical initiative (to roll out all the corporate jargon!). However, several department heads disagree with this new program. They're playing politics by keeping their mouths shut when the CEO is around, but they're also giving you the evil eye and muttering about you to their staff.

You grit your teeth. These are the same people who went to Happy Hour with you last week, yukking it up over beer and black-bean nachos. Now they're undercutting your career.

You could steamroll ahead – after all, you do have the CEO's personal mandate. But you really believe in this project, and you know that these people are thought leaders in the company. What they say directly influences the opinions of the people whose involvement will make or break your success.

So you set aside your frustration, and you talk – and more importantly, you listen. You ask about their concerns. You go out of your way to understand their concerns, and you respond with solutions, not just words. You put plans in place to address each and every issue, and you explicitly check back with them to be sure those plans accurately and completely address their issues.

And then you make very, very sure that the plans are carried out.

The project succeeds, better than you or anyone else expected, because you played *heartfelt, empathetic* politics.

As I said, each of these situations actually happened, to me or to my clients. In understanding them, I hope you're seeing a different perspective on what it means to play politics. Real politics. Not defensive reactions to protect your ego, not convenient, empty words without substance or honesty, not false agreement for the sake of expedience. Real politics: politics with your heart and soul behind them.

That's my definition of politics. I hope you'll come join me on the playground.

Politics in the Office versus Politics Everywhere

As I said above in defining politics, they're everywhere. They are the heart and soul of human interaction.

Yet many of my clients – and perhaps you, too – are surprised to hear that politics even exist outside the office.

Why is it, then, that politics seem so slimy in the office, and virtually un-noticeable outside the office?

Because there's a great deal more at stake when people's jobs are involved – when your job is involved.

If you're very lucky, you enjoy your job; it excites you, and you're continually learning, growing, and contributing.

But even if you hate your job, or – like the majority – just feel basically okay about it, it's still what enables you to put food on the table, a roof over your head, and allows you to live a lifestyle that, while it may or may not be what you imagined or what you aspire to, is still reasonably comfortable and has its extravagances, luxuries, and pleasures.

Or perhaps your lifestyle is even better than you imagined – which means your survival in the workplace is even more significant.

If you're like many people, this includes not only you, but also a spouse or partner and perhaps children or pets who depend on the income your job brings.

You almost certainly have friends and family who live lifestyles similar to yours and whose opinions are important to you.

If you suddenly had no job, whether because you quit, were laid off, or were fired, your lifestyle would change. Those who rely on your income could suffer. You might worry that the people whose opinions are important to you would change those opinions. Your self-image – your identity – would become significantly different.

In your personal life, you can walk away from situations where the people involved don't share your values. You don't make friends with people whose approach to life is uncomfortably different from yours. You don't stick around in community situations – volunteer jobs, church committees, knitting clubs, play groups for your kids, poker buddies, block parties, golf foursomes, and so on – where you feel out of sync with the other people.

But in the office, you don't have the option of walking away. Whether you like someone or not, you still have to work together. If your manager sounds like a used-car salesman when he's trying to get his project approved by senior management, you not only have to keep quiet about your opinion of his behavior, you also have to support his efforts. And how you help, and the extent to which you help, can become one of those battles I describe above, where either your career or your integrity (or both) is held hostage — hostage to your lifestyle and, in many ways, to your survival and your identity.

Therefore, in the office your political skills are tested far more than they are in your personal life. In the office, you're exposed to people whose values, integrity, and definition of politics are not only different from yours, but may be incomprehensible and even offensive to you.

Because your job is at stake, you can feel trapped by political game-playing.

And this is why politics, which are everywhere, feel so disturbingly icky at work, but are almost invisible elsewhere.

At work, you have fewer choices, and there's too much at stake to walk away when things get uncomfortable or difficult.

You have to stay and face the politics.

Shifting the Paradigm

Understanding these concepts — the reality that interpersonal politics exist everywhere, why it feels so much worse at work and is almost unnoticeable outside the office, and what heartfelt, empathetic politics can be like — is the first step toward expanding your view of what politics is.

When you've lived with a point of view for a long time, especially when that point of view involves deeply-held personal beliefs, values, and your sense of integrity, it can be hard to change, and it can feel strangely disorienting when you do begin to change. Your natural tendency is to feel curious and skeptical at the same time.

I'd like to encourage you to fully experience those feelings of curiosity and skepticism, and allow them to invite you to explore this path. Experimenting with my suggestions is the best way for you know if this approach towards politics will work for you.

To begin the process, start with a look at what I call the "Five Deadly *Shoulds*" of office politics. These are the career- and life-wrecking Dragons that every office worker fights at one point or another. In the sections that follow, we'll examine each one in detail, and I'll give you ways to combat them and redeem your career and your self-image from their clutches.

If you've been mired in some of the battles I described above, or if you see yourself caught by the Dragons whose descriptions follow, I urge you to try on this new definition of politics: heartfelt, empathetic politics, politics as the heart and soul of human interaction. It may feel a little weird at first, but if you give it a chance, I think you'll like the way it fits.

Read through the descriptions of each Dragon, think about the case studies, work through the exercises, and try out the suggestions.

You've got nothing to lose – except a hostage situation for your career and your life!

How to Use This Book

Each of the Five Deadly *Shoulds* (Dragons) has its own chapter in which you'll find these sections:

- A summary of how the Dragon operates and its effects on your life and career.
- Examples of beliefs held by people who are hostage to that Dragon, and why those beliefs are unhelpful (and dangerous to your wellbeing and your career).
- A case study describing real examples of people who had their careers damaged by that Dragon.

Following the Five Deadly *Shoulds* chapters is a section of Exercises and Worksheets for each Dragon to help you try out new approaches and see how they fit for you.

A Note on the Case Studies

Each of the case studies is personally known by me to be true. The names are changed to protect everyone concerned.

Let's go fight Dragons!

First Dragon: I Should Be Able to Succeed Without Participating in Office Politics

It may seem as if you have a choice about whether or not to participate in politics in your workplace.

That's an illusion.

When you think you've chosen not to participate, you have instead chosen to abdicate your personal power.

If you think you don't want personal power, think again.

POWER

By "power," I don't mean what some call "power-over," or the ability to "make" people do things. I mean the intrinsic, internal power we all have, whether we choose to use it or not. It's the power of who you are, the power of your skills, abilities, and experience, the power of your heart. It's what creates passion and enthusiasm and builds connection between people.

When you stand in your power, you stand on a firm foundation. From there, you can act with strength, decisiveness, and flexibility.

When you abdicate your power, you stand in quicksand – and it feels like it, too.

See the *Worksheets and Exercises* section of this book for ways to understand and reclaim your personal power.

The greatest leaders – people like Mahatma Gandhi, Mother Teresa, Martin Luther King, and anyone whom you hold as a role model and hero – had (have) great personal power and wielded it with extraordinary political finesse. You may not aspire to being a leader on the world's stage, but you *can* be a true leader within your workplace – *if* you reclaim and retain your personal power.

Two Ways the First Dragon Mangles Your Career

1. When you fail to take the needs and wants of others into account, your strategic plans, your project proposals, and your ideas will be one-dimensional and likely to fail.

I don't mean your project outlines or descriptions won't demonstrate the project's merit.

But if you present a project or idea solely from one perspective (yours), as people who are hostage to this Dragon tend to do, you cannot expect it to stand when you've given it only one leg to balance on.

Creating more legs means, among other things, understanding and including others' perspectives as well as the needs of other teams, departments, and perhaps even other organizations that may be impacted. Then you can build a structure with far more stability, balance, and usefulness.

People who are hostages to this Dragon feel that getting others on board with their ideas, especially if they have to change their original plan in order to do so, is sales-y and phony.

It's not.

The difference lies in your honest desire to understand the wants and needs of other people in other areas. To reach that understanding, you have to ask curious, caring questions and listen to the answers – listen for the deeper meaning, for the answer underneath the answer.

When you incorporate their ideas into your plans, you're being cooperative, collaborative, and even generous. As a side benefit, you'll almost always improve your original ideas.

And there's nothing about used car sales in that approach.

2. When you refuse to identify and interact with the unwritten power structures, you lose out on opportunities to participate, collaborate, and learn.

In families and other social groups, there are always overt leaders (mother, father, perhaps grandparents; official group leaders such as volunteer committee chairs or the softball-team organizer).

Then there are the unspoken leaders who may be ringleaders in trouble-making (little brother Johnny, who gets his older siblings into hot water with his hare-brained ideas) or in inspiration (the volunteer worker who gets everyone passionate about fundraising).

It's the same at work. (I do keep saying that politics are everywhere, don't I?) The obvious leaders – the project managers, program managers, department heads, senior management – are, well, obvious. And then there are the unofficial thought leaders: the people who have won the trust and respect of their peers and management, and whose opinions matter to the success or failure of a project, an individual, and in many ways to the organization as a whole.

Unfortunately, sometimes – depending on how politicized your organization is – these people are political players in a negative sense.

It's easy to tell the difference. When someone is a leader based on intimidation, favoritism, or status rather than respect, leadership, and talent, you have the flip side of the coin, the negative image or evil twin of what true thought leadership should be.

Once you've decided which type you're dealing with, you can find ways to avoid or counteract the negative leaders.

Pay close attention to the positive leaders.

First, understand the role they could play, if you engage with them effectively, in the success of your projects and your career.

Second, you would do well to study them. These positive thought leaders know how to play politics in the best way. The trust and respect they have, and the leadership positions they've achieved (which may or may not include an actual leadership title), are due to their ability to operate politically with compassion and integrity.

Connecting with this unwritten power structure is about getting and giving help, not about being sneaky, sales-y, or gaining unfair advantage.

Case Study

Many years ago, I worked as a software engineer (we called ourselves programmers back then!) in the IT department of a large financial organization. Being reasonably intelligent, productive, and having an ability to communicate in normal English as well as geek-speak, I expected to do well and be rewarded accordingly.

I had come from a tiny services organization where I was one of just five employees. The politics there had been nothing short of astonishing, but I attributed that to the smallness of the organization leading to tremendous jockeying for position and bids for favoritism.

So I blithely set forth into my first big-corporation job believing that politics were behind me and I could simply focus on learning and doing my job.

The people in this financial organization were good and well-meaning. The organization itself was based on sound values and ethical practices. The corporate culture was employee-friendly, with generous benefits and good working conditions.

And fundamentally, I flopped. Others were promoted ahead of me, and my responsibilities and salary quickly got stuck.

My refusal to acknowledge and participate in the unwritten power structures, including correcting my manager's and co-workers' perception of me as a young (true), inexperienced (only partially true), and slightly unreliable (wholly untrue) worker left my career firmly in the talons of the "I should be able to succeed without participating in office politics" Dragon.

I did good work for that organization. I left without being fired, laid off, or even "encouraged" out the door. But in all respects, I failed to advance my career or my self-esteem in any way. I left feeling slighted and ignored. And that feeling was completely accurate: I had been slighted and ignored, because I had abdicated my power. My lack of results were a complete reflection of that abdication.

Second Dragon: I Should Get Recognition for My Work Without Having to Sell Myself.

This is a close relative of the First Dragon, but it's so pervasive and deceptively persuasive that even those who don't succumb to the First Dragon are often taken hostage by the Second Dragon.

It speaks with the voices of your parents and teachers. *Don't boast. Don't brag. Don't show off. Pride goeth before a fall. Virtue is its own reward.*

Boasting, bragging, and showing off are actions based on fear and insecurity.

Owning the real strength and power of your skills and abilities includes letting others know what you can do. (See the note in the First Dragon for an explanation of power in this context.)

Someone may need exactly what you excel at, but how can they find you if you keep it a secret?

You have a responsibility to yourself and to those people who need what you have.

RESPONSIBILITY

Most people look on responsibility as something you accept when you make mistakes. "I take responsibility for what went wrong."

That's the darker side of responsibility, and the smaller side as well.

Truly taking responsibility for the outcomes of your actions and your work means taking responsibility when those outcomes are good as well as when they're bad.

See the *Worksheets and Exercises* section of this workbook for ways to understand more about responsibility.

Two Ways the Second Dragon Mangles Your Career

1. When you do your work so quietly that no one knows whose it is, you get pushed aside and the effort and quality of your work is never recognized or acknowledged.

There's a difference between standing in the strength and power of your skills, talents, individuality, and accomplishments, and "blowing your own horn" in egotistical arrogance.

An artist or a writer doesn't practice false modesty – at least, not if he expects to make a living from his work.

Children are joyfully appreciative of their work – at least, until we socialize their innocent pleasure out of them.

When you're creative and productive in a favorite hobby or sport, you share your enjoyment, appreciation, and success with family and friends.

If you bring that sense of appreciation to work with you, staying alert for opportunities to offer your skills, experience, and accomplishments to help others, you support their efforts with your generosity and talent.

That's a far cry from bragging or arrogant boasting.

2. When you don't stand up to be seen in your busy, productive organization, you cannot come to the attention of the people who need to know about you.

The fact that you and your team are creating the exact reports needed in another department across the building, across the corporate campus, or (in these days of global organizations) across the world, is irrelevant to the person receiving those reports. She wants the reports; that's all. And no matter how much she may appreciate the excellence of the work you've done, if she doesn't know it's yours, she doesn't know to recommend you for a promotion or a transfer into her department – where you might be able to do the exact work you've always dreamed of.

And let's face it, she's way too busy with her own work to hunt you down. It's simply not her responsibility to find you, thank you, or offer recognition and recommendations.

When you move to a new community, you make new connections. That includes finding new doctors, dentists, massage therapists, learning where the best farmers' markets are and the prettiest places to walk or ride your bicycle.

When you know someone in the area, you can ask for a recommendation; when you don't know anyone, you go online to browse local services' web pages.

The people and places you select for these services for yourself and your family are those that present themselves and the quality of their work clearly, with empathy for your problem and a clear statement of their ability to meet your requirements. Their messages create a feeling of recognition and trust within you, and you respond to that by giving them your business.

In the same way, when you create an honest, heartfelt message about who you are and what you stand for, you're as far as you can be from the slick salesperson you might fear becoming. Those who don't need your help in the moment will nonetheless remember your clarity and focus. When they do need your skills, or when someone they work with needs them, they'll remember you and call on you.

Even if they never need you, your reputation will spread and grow. And when people who have never met you know you by reputation, your career is bound to flourish.

This applies, by the way, at all times, whether you're content within your current organization, or job-hunting for a new position.

Case Study

My client Sue spent fifteen years as the Director of Engineering at a technology consulting firm. She specialized in turnarounds, working with the organization's clients to help get their teams and departments back on track and complete their projects.

Her success in this high-stress role was a large factor in the company's success. However, although this position could have been high-profile and highly rewarding as well as high-stress, Sue turned herself and her career over to this Dragon very early on. She felt that her good work was obvious enough to stand on its own merit. Since she wasn't clear in her messages about what she did and how her success helped create the organization's success, when the company was sold she was ill prepared.

A strong, intelligent woman with excellent skills, she nonetheless lost the fight with this Dragon when she became the scapegoat for someone else's bad decisions – and lost her job.

Unfortunately, Sue did what many people who believe in these *shoulds*, or Dragons, do. She repeated her mistake at her next job, and once again was laid off for political reasons.

Since then, however, she's taken on a completely different attitude about her professional credibility. By realizing that she felt fairly confident as long as she was present to explain and protect herself, but completely un-confident about how her reputation might be perceived when she wasn't around, she developed her understanding of what needed to change.

And then Sue did what so few people do: she followed through on her understanding, creating a powerful message of credibility and reputation that carried her forward with confidence and far greater success.

THIRD DRAGON: I SHOULD BE ABLE TO TRUST MY FRIENDS AT WORK TO HAVE MY BEST INTERESTS AT HEART.

It's human nature to want to socialize, to want to interact on a friendly basis with others, to want to trust the people you spend time with. And employee-engagement studies confirm that the more friends and wider network employees have at work, the happier and more engaged they are in their jobs.

However, when you assume that friendship with co-workers is the same as friendship with others outside the workplace, this Dragon can cause your job, if not your career, to get singed.

Your friends at work have desires, needs, hopes, and fears about their career that can cause them to behave differently than they might wish to, or than they might with friends outside the office. (So, I might add, do you!) So take care to remember the sometimes-challenging context within which office friendships form.

TRUST

Trust is a direct result of integrity; without integrity, there simply isn't trust.

Many believe that trust is outside of their control: one either has it, or one doesn't.

In fact, although it can be difficult to regain betrayed trust, trust can be managed (and even regained), as long as you come from a place of integrity, honesty, and compassion.

Notice that trust doesn't have anything to do with friendship. You can trust someone you dislike, and mistrust someone you love.

See the *Worksheets and Exercises* section of this workbook for ways to understand more about trust.

Two Ways the Third Dragon Mangles Your Career

1. When you handle in-office friendships the same way as your out-of-office friendships, you make yourself vulnerable to betrayal.

One of the key indicators of success, happiness, and engagement at work is the strength of your in-house network.

So of course you'll form friendships at work.

And yet, just as politics are different in the workplace versus outside the office, so too are relationships, and for the same reasons.

Outside the office, you expect your friends and partners to stand by you. That, after all, is what friendship and love are all about: steadfastness, loyalty, reliability, caring. Your friends comfort you in bad times and help you celebrate the good times. Whether it's the big promotions, the tough projects, or the lost clients, they're there to cheer, laugh, cry, and groan with you.

Inside the office, the stakes are different, relationships unfold in different ways, and it's a rare friend who will jeopardize his own career for the sake of friendship.

The friend in the office next door may be aiming for the same project or promotion you are. Your friend and co-worker today could be your manager – or your employee – tomorrow.

The difficult reality is that when it comes to someone's career survival versus your friendship, most people, however regretfully, will go with her own survival.

That goes for you as a friend of others in the office as well as for them as your friends. To what extent would you go to bat for a workplace friend, knowing it could have serious repercussions to your career? (It's easy, as you read this, to think indignantly, "But of course I would!" – but when the real-world situation arises, things tend to look a bit different.)

2. When you believe you need to form friendships in order to build trust at work, you end up associating with people you wouldn't necessarily choose to be with outside the office.

It seems at first glance that the least political way to build trust is to build friendships. After all, you trust (and receive trust from) your friends, right?

However, this often means forming "friendships" with people you wouldn't necessarily choose as friends in social situations.

And the reality is that your boss – and her boss, on up the line – will form opinions about you based on their opinions of the people you associate with, and they'll trust you (or not) accordingly. It's a case of guilt (or virtue) by association, of course, and it's also very real.

Associate yourself with thought leaders and top performers, and you'll be viewed as smart, capable, and trustworthy.

Associate yourself with nay-sayers and trouble-makers, and you'll be viewed accordingly.

Case Study

Kim was a successful and respected department manager at a medium-sized software company.

When a position came open in her organization, he did what many do: knowing someone whose qualifications and qualities were a great fit, he hired a friend, Beth.

So far so good; there's nothing inherently dangerous or wrong about this, it happens all the time, and usually has good results for the individuals and the organization. And of course it's why a strong personal network is key in a successful job search.

Unfortunately, due to circumstances beyond their control, an ugly rumor started about Beth's past. Incited by gossip and underhanded nastiness of several other employees, the rumor reached the ears of the CEO, who immediately took steps to fire Beth.

Kim went to bat for his friend, and met with the CEO and Vice President of the company. The discussion got heated, with Kim making what he later admitted to me was a very unfortunate statement: "This isn't a good place to work any more."

Beth was still gone, and Kim was laid off a year later, after leading his department to one of the best years it had ever had. Of course, no one ever said anything except that it was a restructuring of the organization, but there's little doubt in his mind – or mine – that it was because of (a) his actions in defending Beth in the first place, and (b) the heated and unfortunate discussion that ensued.

Had Kim kept his wits about him, he might have been able to stand up for what he felt was right, and still might – or might not – have salvaged his job and standing within the organization. The reality was that Beth's was doomed regardless.

And while we're on the subject of relationships – what about romance in the office?

Let's be honest here: when you enter into a romantic relationship with a co-worker, the possibility for personal and professional pain rises.

If you've never gone down this path and had it end badly, you probably believe you can handle it. And perhaps you can. However, there are some key points to consider.

- It's not a secret. No matter how much you may believe no one notices that you're dating someone in the office, it's not a secret. It's especially not a secret if either of you is already married or in another committed relationship.

- Know your company's policies on relationships between employees. Many organizations frown on committed couples, whether married or not, working in the same department; virtually none will tolerate them in a reporting relationship, and for good reasons.

- Be clear about what conflicts of interest may arise. If you're certain this is the love of your life, I'm thrilled for you – and, plan ahead, together, for how you'll manage questions, concerns, and accusations of favoritism and nepotism. Which of you will find another job, if it becomes necessary?
- From the standpoint of financial safety, remember that both your jobs are at risk if the company runs into trouble. If you're both laid off, what happens?
- What happens if you break up? Can you face the prospect of having to see each other every workday, possibly continuing to work together on the same team and the same projects? A key difference between relationships in the workplace and relationships outside the office is that outside the office, you don't ever have to see each other again if the relationship goes sour. (Of course, this is not the case if you're divorcing and/or you have children, but you see my point.)

I'm not saying "don't ever get involved with someone at work." There are many lovely success stories about beautiful, romantic, lasting relationships that began – and continued – in the office. Just recognize the risk factors, and take steps – as with any risk factor – to manage them in ways you can both live with if things do go wrong.

Fourth Dragon: It Should Be Safe For Me To Tell The Truth.

The truth.

Isn't that what we've been talking about, when we talk about integrity? Isn't truth the cornerstone of integrity, and isn't telling the truth key to upholding our personal value system?

Isn't truth one of the first things to go when the politics get intense and people start mis-using political power?

And if all this is, well, *true*, then why are so few people in an organization ready, willing, and able to tell the truth – and why are there so many consequences for doing so?

This Dragon has all the logical arguments in the world. It can argue up one side and down the other, pointing at the dangers of telling the truth despite the premium we all put on honesty. It has all the statistics: how often the messenger is shot, how project managers and team leads don't want to hear about reality, how managers refuse to listen.

When you yield to this Dragon, you're doing more than handing over your career as a hostage; you're handing over your integrity and self-image.

TRUTH

There's an ancient Chinese saying that there are three truths in any situation: my truth, your truth, and the truth.

From this starting point, you can become curious about the other person's truth, and see how it matches up with yours.

However, as intriguing as this statement is, it doesn't go far enough. The real issue is often that your truth may be something quite different from your manager's or co-worker's (or friend's or family member's).

Which means you need to spend time finding the point of collaboration: the third truth where you can come to agreement.

See the *Worksheets and Exercises* section of this workbook for ways to understand other people's truth and how to combine their truth with yours to create something bigger, more real, and much more useful

Two Ways the Fourth Dragon Mangles Your Career

1. When there's bad news to be told – the project is going to be late, sales aren't meeting expectations, or a key client is delaying – no one wants to be the one to step up and tell the truth for fear of being shot as the messenger.

Let's take a look at an example to see how this works.

The project is going to be late. Someone needs to tell the project manager. No one wants to be the person who steps up to say that no matter how many extra people you put on the job, no matter how many extra hours everyone works, it's just not going to meet the schedule or quality expectations.

The project team's truth is that given the current scope of work, the schedule is impossible.

From their perspective, it seems that this *should* be everyone's truth. But let's take a look at the project manager's truth.

The project manager may be all too aware that the schedule is unrealistic. However, she may feel that her job is on the line. So her truth could be that she wants to keep her job.

Truth: given the current scope of work, the schedule is not realistic.

Truth: the project manager wants to keep her job

Of course, the third truth – the real truth – is that *both* of these are true. The reason the project team's messenger is going to be shot, however, is that – unless they understand politics – they aren't paying attention to the project manager's truth, since they're wholly focused on their own truth.

It's worth noticing that the project team's truth goes beyond their concerns about the schedule. There are individual truths among the team members that have to do with wanting to spend time with family, being concerned about health and stress and burnout, and, yes, being concerned for their own jobs as well.

Only when all the truths – yours, mine, and the intersection of them – are openly considered can you reach a conclusion that will really work.

2. When there's a right way to do things that will produce the results required, but the client is pushing for speed over functionality, you're at risk of appearing opinionated, stubborn, and politically blind.

A commitment to usefulness, quality, and sustainability is a good thing, right? It seems difficult to believe, but this is actually one of the sneakiest ways this Dragon carries off your career. And for people who yield to this Dragon, it's a frustrating, bewildering, and painful experience.

This is a case where the truth that needs to be told is the difficult truth to yourself, not the other person. As is the case for most issues concerning this Dragon, the conflict is between two people's truths – in this case, the client's truth and your truth. (Every project or task has a "client" – the stakeholder, the person, team, or group that will receive the finished outcome, your manager, and so forth. That stakeholder may be external or internal to your organization; my use of the word "client" is intended to represent the person, team, or department who receives your finished product or service and/or the person to whom you and your team report.)

Let's assume you've done a good job explaining why your plan is best, and you've explained all the potential risks and drawbacks of the client's plan. They haven't changed their minds. If that's the case, then their truth, as the intended recipient of the outcomes, becomes *the* truth in this situation.

It's not a case of "the customer is always right," because we all know that the customer is *not* always right. It's a reality (a truth) of business, however, that sometimes good enough is exactly that – good enough – even though "good enough" may be in conflict with your truth about excellence and quality.

Case Study

Many years ago, I was the Director of Professional Services at a software development company. I was responsible for ensuring that my team of project managers and consultants met our customers' systems implementation needs.

Joe was one of my best technical people. He's smart, talented, and determined – and he was stubborn, opinionated, and politically blind. Customers loved him because his expertise and confidence were obvious to them; they *knew* he could and would get the job done.

However, Joe had a tremendously difficult time when a client wanted something done in a way he disagreed with. Joe knew how things should be in order for them to be top quality, and anything less than that was more than annoying; it was deeply disturbing to him. You could see the stress filling him up, tensing his shoulders and jaw, tightening his walk, till sometimes I expected him to shatter into little pieces with the strain.

So Joe got himself into a number of situations where his truth – the truth of how things should be in order to be excellent – collided head-on with the client's truth – the truth that they needed to accept less functionality and sometimes even less quality for greater speed.

Fortunately for Joe's career, some help from me and his co-workers and a little more experience helped him understand that sometimes the business truth has to trump the technological truth. I don't think he'll ever be happy about this, but he's grown much better at knowing how to discern the various truths in a situation, when to push his case, and when to accept alternatives.

FIFTH DRAGON: SENIOR MANAGEMENT SHOULD ALWAYS KNOW WHAT THEY'RE DOING.

It seems reasonable to expect that, by the time someone has reached a senior management or executive position, they'll be confident, experienced, decisive, reasonable, intuitive, knowledgeable, able to leap tall buildings in a single bound – oh, wait, that's Superman.

This Dragon leads you into overblown expectations and therefore inevitable disappointment. When you expect your managers and senior executives to be super-human, you fall into a whole series of traps that create frustration, put roadblocks in your way, and can easily undermine your career.

COURAGE

It takes courage to put your ideas forward to people who are senior to you, and it *really* takes courage to stand up and speak out when something's going wrong or your opinion might be unpopular with your co-workers, employees, or management.

Fortunately, there are ways to make it easier on yourself as well as to protect yourself from the potential fallout.

See the *Worksheets and Exercises* section of this workbook for ways to understand more about courage — especially what I call "smart courage."

Managers and leaders at any level of any organization are human. A lot of the time, they're flying by the seat of their pants just like the rest of us.

So you might experiment with what it's like to have some compassion for your management team. They're scared sometimes, just like you. They're confused sometimes, just like you. They put their socks on one foot a time, just like you. And even the best leaders have bad days.

Two Ways the Fifth Dragon Mangles Your Career

1. When you expect leaders to be fully responsible for taking the organization, department, or team in the right direction, you risk of abdicating your own responsibility.

Employees, including managers, trust their leaders to take the company in the right direction. As we know all too well, however, that doesn't always happen. (Think Enron, Arthur Anderson, Kodak, Lehman Brothers ... the list goes on!)

As children, and even as teenagers and young adults, you rely on the authority figures in life — parents, teachers, other family members and adult family friends — to cope with the difficult decisions, to help you understand what's right and what's wrong, to care for you. You rely on these people for physical, emotional, and ethical survival.

As an adult, though most likely as a fairly young and immature adult, you entered the political world of work. A *BusinessWeek* special report, "The Future of Work," included the amusing statistic that 6% of office workers under 30 admitted they'd accidentally called their bosses "mom" or "dad." Whether you've ever made that slip or not, there's a telling truth here: it's easy, natural almost, to allow your organization's leadership to take on that familiar authority figure/caretaker role.

Put down in black and white like this, it's obviously a fallacy. Your managers and the organization's executive team have responsibility for their own careers and for the work done by their individual areas. They're not responsible for your career, for maintaining your sense of right and wrong, or for your survival.

When you take responsibility for your career, your integrity, and your survival within the organization, you're stepping into your personal power. When you step into your personal power, you can take action – political and otherwise – with integrity and compassion. Then *you* become a leader – whether or not you hold a leadership title or role – able to participate in the decisions and actions that guide the company's future.

It's a much more enjoyable place to be, and far more likely to lead to your career success.

2. When your managers are protective of their authority, unwilling to listen to others' ideas, or stuck in a rut of "how we've always done things," influencing their ideas and decisions is difficult and risky.

This is where politics comes into its own – and where politics gets a big part of its bad reputation.

It's no secret that people have different personal styles, whether that's how they get their work done (focused and methodical, or multitasking wildly); how they prefer to communicate (all email all the time, face to face, or on the phone); how they want to hear bad news (never, with abject apologies, or with plenty of suggestions and data backup); how they prefer to keep informed (details, details, details, or just the high-point bullets, please); and so forth.

You know this, but how often do you actually *act* on that knowledge? And it's acting on this knowledge that allows you to influence different people in different ways, each according to your observations about their individual style.

When your friend Amy calls to bemoan the latest disaster that her son Johnny has gotten into, you know she just wants you to listen, groan in the right places, laugh in the right places. You know, because you know her, that right now she needs to blow off steam. She's already dealt with Johnny, and won't appreciate your suggestions for how to help Johnny stay out of trouble. So even though you just met someone who specializes in working with gifted but troublesome kids like Johnny, you keep your mouth shut – for now. In a day or two, you'll drop her an email, and then maybe give her a call sometime next week to follow up.

That's politics at play (heartfelt and empathetic), even though you probably made those choices without consciously noticing how you were sifting through a whole host of clues, such as the tone in Amy's voice, the words she was using to tell her story, what you know about how she receives new ideas, her territorial tendencies as a parent, and your own desire to help.

You study your friends and family because you love them and want to know them better. You have a different relationship with your manager, and you probably don't exert the same type of effort in understanding them.

Nonetheless, if you consciously take the time to study your manager – and your co-workers, employees, and as many of the senior management team as you have access to – you'll reap amazing rewards.

Your understanding of what motivates people, of their professional and personal needs, are the key to becoming truly proficient at heartfelt, empathetic politics.

Case Study

Business consultants like Louise often have an amazing network of reporting structures to navigate. Louise reported to a total of four different people: two within her consulting organization (her own boss, plus the client's account manager) and two more at the client organization.

Initially, this made her a little crazy because of all the different things each person wanted. "It was a full-time job keeping up with all the communication, never mind the work I was hired to do!"

However, by paying attention, *asking curious questions* (something most people seldom do), listening to the answers (and listening for what wasn't said as well as what was said), and responding to their reactions, Louise learned what each of them really wanted, and incorporated that into her schedule. She saved time by not having to re-do work for them (since she knew exactly what they wanted), and she gained a reputation for reliability and responsiveness with all four.

Exercises and Worksheets

Introduction

By now, you've noticed that each of the five Dragons – the five *shoulds* we all tend to believe but which are likely to sabotage your career, sooner or later – also introduced a personal quality that will help you pursue your career with dignity and integrity.

- Power
- Responsibility
- Trust
- Truth
- Courage

You may be surprised to find these concepts discussed in a book dealing with office politics. If so, that surprise probably stems from your accepting the biggest "should" of them all, what I call the Fundamental Misconception:

The Fundamental Misconception

Office politics is sleazy, underhanded, and deceitful.

It's all about people's egos and who you backstab or brown-nose to get ahead.

It doesn't matter how good your work is, because the winner is the one who's best at playing the game, not the one doing the best work.

As you've seen in looking at each of the Five Deadly *Shoulds*, each of the three statements in the Fundamental Misconception *can have* validity. With office politics just as with any tool, there's a dark side, characterized by abuse and misuse.

And just as with any tool, there's a bright side, characterized by creativity, integrity, compassion, empathy, and heart.

The bright side of office politics revolves around these five concepts of Power, Responsibility, Trust, Truth, and Courage.

In this section, I'll go into more detail about what these concepts mean in terms of office politics, and how you can use your understanding to change your approach and become more successful – and more at peace with yourself and comfortable within your integrity.

Take the time to read through the discussion of each concept, because it will almost certainly be a bit different from what you're used to. You may want to give yourself time between reading each discussion and the next, and also between reading each discussion and going through the worksheet questions and exercises.

In fact, I recommend at least a day's observation and processing time for each, which will help you see how your current definition of each concept affects what you do, and think about how the different definition might create better results.

Then you can use what you've learned during the time of observation to help answer the questions and internalize the exercises.

You'll find it useful to have a partner or even to work in a group as you go through the exercises. Of course, I don't necessarily recommend partnering with co-workers (see the Third Dragon for some reasons why!). But you could get together with friends who are in similar stages of their careers and support each other through these exercises. You'll find bigger insights and better results when you have others' input and the opportunity to give them your feedback as well.

However you choose to work through this section, enjoy yourself! The wonderful thing about this new way of looking at office politics is that it truly can be joyful and fun.

Politics is really about working within the process to do what needs to be done – working with my peers, my team, and my management to move the company forward without stepping on anyone else's toes. It's about how to form a team and be a leader even when the company's leadership isn't making the effort. More importantly, it's how to do all that while caring for the success of everyone.
~ *Paul Jones, Resources Development Manager, San Diego, CA*

What could be more fun than that?

Power

When someone says "power" to you, what do you think of?

The ability to "make" someone do something? Control? Authority? Dictatorships?

The Roman philosopher Seneca wrote, "Most powerful is he who has himself in his own power."

A New Definition

In the discussion of the First Dragon, "I *should* be able to succeed without participating in office politics," I introduced a new way of looking at and experiencing power.

POWER

By "power," I don't mean what some call "power-over," or the ability to "make" people do things. I mean the intrinsic, internal power we all have, whether we choose to use it or not. It's the power of who you are, the power of your skills, abilities, and experience, the power of your heart. It's what creates passion and enthusiasm and builds connection between people.

When you stand in your power, you stand on a firm foundation. From there, you can act with strength, decisiveness, and flexibility.

When you abdicate your power, you stand in quicksand – and it feels like it, too.

We generally view power as something that we acquire through outside authority or special expertise, and we generally view it as "power over."

A police officer has *power over* the public because of his or her job and the edict of law.

A manager has *power over* employees because of his or her title and position in the organization.

A parent has *power over* his children because children are helpless at birth and need guidance and support for many years.

A doctor or other specialized expert has *power over* her patients (or clients) because of accumulated knowledge and expertise.

And so forth.

Sometimes, this *power over* hierarchy results from abdication rather than outside authority.

One person in a relationship might abdicate power to the other, giving up *power over* his activities, thoughts, and emotions.

An employee might abdicate power to her manager, giving up *power over* her career, quality of life, and ethical choices.

An adult may abdicate power (by never claiming their role as an adult) to a parent, giving up *power over* his life choices and happiness.

You might abdicate your power to the various Dragons in various ways.

You yield power to authentic authority, but you might abdicate your power to inauthentic or perceived authority.

You exercise your power – or not – in the ways you respond to people, how you wield your own authority, and perhaps even in passive-aggressive behavior.

With all of that said, the truest power anyone can have is the power of self, as Seneca said so many years ago.

When you stand in the fullness of your own personal power, you're on the firmest foundation you can experience. Acting from that foundation, you are strong, decisive, and flexible.

In Action

For the next several days or a week (or the rest of your life!), be an observer of power. See how the people around you, at work and outside, accept, assume, or abdicate power.

What can you learn from your observations?

Some of what you learn may be ways to improve, and some may be recognition of bad habits you share.

After you've observed for a while, complete the worksheet and exercise below. Then take your new understanding out into the world and observe some more.

How does this new feeling of personal power change your interactions with others? How do they react when you're acting from the foundation of your personal power? What sort of impact are you making on the world with this different definition of power? And how do you feel about yourself?

Worksheet

1. How do you feel about power?

You've read the definitions, you've read how power plays its part in each of the Five Deadly *Shoulds*, and you've seen how the Dragons steal power. You've taken the time to observe your co-workers, employees, and management; your family and friends; and the people in line and on duty in the grocery store, bank, or dry cleaners.

What observations do you have now about power and how it operates in life and business?

(**Example**: I'm surprised and a little sad at the ways I see people abdicate their power, and the ways in which society seems to require that we do so. I noticed, too, how I sometimes give up my own power just because it seems easier in the moment. I let someone else make an important project decision at work, for instance. It seemed natural, until I suddenly noticed what had happened, and then it just felt weird.)

2. How is this different from how you felt before?

Notice how your views on power have shifted, even if only a little bit. Noticing how change happens is important in recognizing how you change, and understanding how to continue to change.

(**Example**: Well, before I never, I mean never, thought about power. Or if I did, it was just in the "power over" ways you've discussed. Can my manager "make" me work overtime, is the cop on the corner going to notice that I just rolled through that stop sign, that kind of thing. I must say, it's a little uncomfortable to be noticing power in this new way!)

3. Can you identify ways in which you may have abdicated your power?

(**Example**: You don't ask easy questions, do you? All right, yes, of course I recognize ways I've been abdicating my power. It starts with letting my manager schedule a conflicting meeting last week, and it goes on from there to things like feeling pressured to produce those reports before I had all the data I wanted. Ugh. And I can see the fallout from each of these abdications, too: the meeting I had to skip in order to attend my manager's meeting turned out to be important, and the data that was missing from the report meant I had to re-issue the report with corrections, which doesn't reflect well on my competence.)

Exercise: Step Into Your Power of Self

If you're not used to this type of thing, this exercise may feel a little strange. Don't worry – no one (except you) will ever know that you did it!

Having said that, and as I mentioned above, it's helpful to do these exercises with someone else. It's fun to trade exercises with friends in similar situations in their work, and it's helpful to get someone else's feedback, coaching, and support.

Exercise

Stand up. (Really. I'll wait.)

Close your eyes. (This is just one reason why it's useful to have someone guide you through the exercise.)

Think about your successes, the things you consider to be your triumphs. Think about the experiences you've gathered, the failures you've learned from and mourned, the successes you've learned from and celebrated, and all your skills, talents, and abilities.

Think of specific instances when you were in full swing, in the flow, doing what you do best and being brilliant at it.

Don't limit yourself to work-related experiences; bring it all in.

Feel it. Remember what you were thinking and how you were feeling, and really experience how it felt in your body. Were you smiling? Laughing? How did your gut feel? Your heart? How were you standing? Stand like that now. Re-experience these feelings in yourself.

This is your personal power, and it's glorious.

Now draw an imaginary circle around yourself. See this circle becoming a bubble, and you're standing inside it. Feel the bubble around you, containing all these memories of your experience and your feelings of *power*.

Create a door in the bubble and open it. Open your eyes and step out of the door – literally, step forwards. You will feel those feelings, that sense of personal power in your experiences, drop away as you step through the door.

Turn around. Even though it was imaginary, you know where the bubble is. Step back into it, and you'll feel that sense of strength, certainty, and power drop right back over you.

Step out and, in your mind's eye, fold up the bubble into a package, and store it away.

Now you know where it is, and you can open it up and step into it any time you need it.

Next time you're facing a difficult conversation, a tough meeting, or you need to talk about your work and your abilities in ways that haven't felt comfortable up till now, you can open up that bubble in your mind's eye, step into it (literally step forwards into it), and feel that *power of self* all over again.

RESPONSIBILITY

So, what do you think of when you think about responsibility?

"Owning up" to doing something wrong, having made a mistake? Taking on the weight of everyone else's mistakes when you lead a project team or a department? Picking up all the tasks that no one else seems to be doing … to be "taking responsibility" for?

Bob Dylan said, "I think of a hero as someone who understands the degree of responsibility that comes with his freedom."

A New Definition

I introduced this concept of *responsibility* in the chapter on the Second Dragon, "I *should* get recognition for my work without having to sell myself."

RESPONSIBILITY

Most people look on *responsibility* as something you accept when you make mistakes. "I take responsibility for what went wrong."

That's the darker side of responsibility, and the smaller side as well.

Truly taking responsibility for the outcomes of your actions and your work means taking responsibility when those outcomes are good as well as when they're bad.

Responsibility has acquired an undeservedly challenging reputation. From childhood, we're *held responsible* for the mistakes we make. As managers, we're *held responsible* for the actions of our project teams and departments. More specifically, we're told that to be good managers and leaders we must *accept responsibility* for our team's mistakes while passing on credit for their successes. And rightly so; this is indeed the task of the manager and leader.

But the focus seems always to be on the mistakes that people make, whether our own or those of the people we lead. Whatever happened to the idea that we are equally responsible for "owning up to" our successes?

Going back to Dylan's comment above, freedom – which is based on personal power – does indeed imply great responsibility. And that responsibility means publicly acknowledging the things you do *well* at least as much as it means publicly acknowledging where you screwed up.

This isn't bragging, boasting, or arrogance. And it's also not false modesty, or what I call the "aw, shucks" shuffle, when we disingenuously try to say that "it was nothing."

In Action

Spend some time observing how you and those around you respond to success. Do you take responsibility for it, or do you do an "aw, shucks, t'weren't nuthin'" shuffle? Do you step into your personal power, feeling and believing in your success, and being clear about what you've done, or do you neglect to own the reality of your effort and your results?

What about the people around you? How are they expressing their responsibility? Do they acknowledge their success, or is it only their mistakes they shoulder?

Once you've had time to observe, complete the worksheet below and try out the exercise.

Worksheet

1. How do you feel about responsibility?

You've read the definition, you've read how responsibility plays its part in each of the Five Deadly *Shoulds*, and you've seen how the Dragon tempts you to take responsibility only for your mistakes. You've watched the reactions of managers, co-workers, employees; family and friends; and those in the businesses you patronize.

What observations do you have now about responsibility and how it operates in life and business?

(**Example**: I don't know many people who take responsibility for success, and I find that a little – no, a lot – startling. I see so many people, myself included, who can't accept compliments without pointing out the flaws in whatever is being praised, who "blame" all their success on luck and all their failure on themselves. I'm surprised at how I never noticed that before, and it makes me feel very sad.

When I contrast this behavior to my mom, who always enjoyed being up-front about what she did and – now that I think of it – was very successful at almost everything she did, it really shows me how empowering it can be to take responsibility for the good things as well as the mistakes, and how success naturally results from that.)

2. How is this different from how you felt before?

Notice how your views about responsibility have shifted, even if only a little bit. Noticing how change happens is important in recognizing how you change, and understanding how to continue to change.

(**Example**: I always thought that was the way it was supposed to be – being self-effacing, modest, all that, and making sure that I took responsibility – uh, blame! – for my mistakes. I heard someone say once, when she was complimented on a job well done, "Thank you – you're right!" and I practically got whiplash doing a double-take. Wow. How cool is that, to have such confidence! So maybe I need to start cultivating some of that confidence myself.)

3. How can you take responsibility differently now than in the past?

(**Example**: I'm going to look at what I've done and have some respect for my own abilities and the results I produce. And when someone compliments me, I'm going to squelch all my tendencies to say, "But you missed this mistake," or, "Well, thanks, but it wasn't that big a deal," or anything like that. I may have to bite the tip of my tongue right off, but I'm going to stop saying those things. For one thing – people might actually believe that my hard work really *isn't* a big deal, and that would *not* be true!)

Exercise: Acknowledge Your Excellence

For this exercise, you don't have to do any visualization or even stand up from your chair.

What you do need is at least an hour of uninterrupted time (two hours is better), a good pen (everyone has a favorite pen), and a nice notebook or good-quality pad of paper.

I strongly advise that you do this exercise in longhand on paper, *not* on your computer. When you actually physically write, using materials that are pleasing to you, it has a great deal more significance, power, and impact.

Exercise

Start by making a list of the last five things – or more, if you like – that you completed. These should be reasonably significant projects, not something simple like "Mowed the lawn" or "Went to work."

Perhaps you'll list work-related projects, such as a complex report you completed, or a project milestone you reached successfully. Or they could be personal projects – a craft project completed, a truly excellent round of golf, mentoring your oldest child to step into her own personal power.

Whatever you select, these should be things you feel you did a good job on and which you feel pride in completing.

List them one to a page in your notebook or on your pad of paper.

Your next step is to write down what you think was the best thing about the project. What makes it stand out for you? What's particularly satisfying about it? What did you do that made it work well, that made it a success?

Enjoy yourself with this. You're writing just for you. Have fun. Appreciate your good work. Be thorough!

Now, in the space left on the page (or take a new page if you need more room), write the names of three people who are aware of the completed project *and* who know what a good job you did on it. If at all possible, pick people you're comfortable with – if not friends, at least friendly acquaintances. Put their names at intervals, equally spaced down the page.

Underneath each name, write down what you think each of them would say was best about the project. Since you're basically fantasizing here, you don't need to be as thorough as you were when writing your own thoughts. A bullet list is fine.

Now comes the fun part!

Walk down the hall or around the block or pick up the phone – whatever it takes to actually get in touch with these people. Face-to-face is ideal, on the phone is okay; this is not an exercise to conduct by email.

Ask what they thought was good about the project.

Don't ask what you could improve. This is not a project post-mortem (and what a dreadful name that is for a project review!). Nor is it a time for constructive feedback or a continuous-improvement process. Both of those are great in their place, but that's not what this is about.

Ask what you did that was good.

If this seems really hard, pick one person on your list whom you know well. Brainstorm some ways to ask. For instance, "I'm curious about your opinion on something. You know that project I just finished? Well, I tried out this new way of doing *xyz*, and I thought it worked out really well. What do you think?"

It's easier than you think. And I'll wager you'll get some eye-opening insight into what you do well.

Trust

Do you feel as if trust is an "either/or" thing – you either have the trust of your colleagues, or you don't?

I've seen long discussions of trust waged on various discussion forums. Most people believe it's intangible, something that you can neither measure nor manage.

However, Stephen M.R. Covey (son of Stephen R. Covey of FranklinCovey fame) writes in his book *The Speed of Trust* that, "We can increase trust – much faster than we might think – and doing so will have a huge impact, both in the quality of our lives and in the results we're able to achieve." He goes on to say, "The ability to grow, extend, and restore trust with all stakeholders...is *the* key leadership competency of the new global economy."

A New Definition

In the Third Dragon, "I *should* be able to trust that my friends at work have my best interests at heart," I wrote about managing trust – something most people think can't be done.

TRUST

Trust is a direct result of integrity; without integrity, there simply isn't trust.

Many believe that trust is outside of their control: one either has it, or one doesn't.

In fact, although it can be difficult to regain betrayed trust, trust can be managed (and even regained), as long as you come from a place of integrity, honesty, and compassion.

Notice that trust doesn't have anything to do with friendship. You can trust someone you dislike, and mistrust someone you love.

So what is this notion of *managing* trust? How can you possibly manage whether someone trusts you or not?

By going through the *power* and *responsibility* steps in this Exercises and Worksheets section of the book, you're already taking steps to do so.

When you step into and up to your *personal power*, you operate from a solid foundation of who you are. When your actions are aligned with that foundation, you build credibility, which leads to trust.

Combining that with taking responsibility for *all* outcomes of your work, the good and the bad, means you're transmitting a consistent message about your work and its quality, as well as your ability and willingness to stand for that quality. You are whole and undivided within yourself, which is what *integrity* really means. And this transmits credibility and trustworthiness.

Bearing this in mind, you'll naturally begin to see other ways in which you can build your reputation and credibility (i.e., trustworthiness) in the eyes of others.

In Action

Observe how people you work and play with respond to your new behaviors in the realm of *power* and *responsibility.*

Take some time to observe and think about how your feelings of trust for others change depending on the situation and on what – if anything – they do to manage your trust in them. If you're interacting with someone who abdicates his personal power, how does that affect your trust for him? Likewise, if someone is matter-of-fact and up-front – *responsible* – about the quality of her work, how do you respond?

Worksheet

1. How do you feel about trust?

You've read the definitions and you've read how trust – misplaced or lack thereof – plays its part in each of the Five Deadly *Shoulds.* You've watched the reactions of managers, co-workers, employees; family and friends; people in businesses you admire, and businesses you don't choose to patronize.

What observations do you have now about trust and how it operates in life and business?

(**Example**: I think I've always viewed trust as black and white – either I trusted someone and they trusted me, or not. I'm beginning to see how it's really shades of grey, and how it can vary depending on the situation. And I can also see that other people's trust in me can be responsive to what I do. That's very interesting and very encouraging!)

2. How is this different from how you felt before?

Notice how your views about trust have shifted, even if only a little bit. Noticing how change happens is important in recognizing how you change, and understanding how to continue to change.

(**Example**: Well, I always thought of trust as very on/off, yes/no, black/white. I never considered what specific – and surprisingly practical – ways there are to increase others' perception of my trustworthiness. And I can see how this is practicing politics with integrity, because I don't think it would be possible to manipulate this "management of trust" thing – someone's real motivations would show themselves very quickly.)

3. What can you do right now to start building your own trustworthiness?

(**Example**: Well, I'm going to go back to the exercises on Power and Responsibility and take another look at them. It's important to me that my manager and co-workers trust me, so I'm excited about the idea of being able to legitimately and authentically increase their trust in me!

Also, I'm beginning see how I've been abdicating responsibility for how much faster we're responding to customer service inquiries about shipment status on orders. The improvements are completely due to my decision to consolidate the order-tracking systems, and I've been doing what you called the "aw shucks shuffle" on that. It's time I stood up and said, *This* is what I did, and these are the results of it. That feels really good!)

Exercise: Manage your Trust Foundation

Understanding how to manage others' trust in you, and taking action to do so, are skills you've been learning in the previous two sections.

In the discussion of the Third Dragon, I wrote about how trust forms on a foundation of integrity, personal power, and responsibility.

When you act from integrity, fully stepping into your personal power, and stepping up to responsibility for the outcomes of *all* your actions, people will trust you – in direct proportion to their sense of how firm your foundation really is.

Exercise

So the exercise for Trust is to go back and review your worksheets and exercises for Power and Responsibility. Consider your answers, consider the extent to which you completed the exercises and then took action in your workplace based on those exercises, and see if you can extend yourself a little further and a little deeper in those areas.

Truth

Many people claim to know what "the truth" is.

It's my contention that we can only ever know our own truth. However, that's a discussion for a philosophy treatise, not a book on office politics!

Sir Arthur Conan Doyle's Sherlock Holmes says, "When you have eliminated the impossible, whatever remains, however impossible, must be the truth." With that in mind, I encourage you to open your horizons and see how useful this new idea of multiple truths can be to you and your success.

A New Definition

The Fourth Dragon, "It *should* be safe for me to tell the truth," introduced what I think is the most powerful and u*seful* definition of *truth* I've come across.

TRUTH

There's an ancient Chinese saying that there are three truths in any situation: my truth, your truth, and the truth.

From this starting point, you can become curious about the other person's truth, and see how it matches up with yours.

However, as intriguing as this statement is, it doesn't go far enough. The real issue is often that your truth may be something quite different from your manager's or co-worker's (or friend's or family member's).

Which means you need to spend time finding the point of collaboration: the third truth where you can come to agreement.

Truth is a loaded term for a lot of people. It carries a lot of cultural significance – maybe more than any of the other qualities we've discussed here.

Yet, as I said above, this isn't the place for a weighty philosophical discussion of *truth*. Instead, I'd like to request that if the government-political significance of truth is bugging you, or if the religious aspect of the idea of truth is making it hard to look at it in this different way, or if it's the heated debate you had last night with your kids about the truth of who did what to whom, please know that I understand all that.

The definition I propose here has so much value that I'm asking you to set those questions aside and think about what this way of looking at truth might do for your career and your success.

Think of it as a useful tool rather than the *truth* about truth!

In Action

Look around you over the next few days and notice the ways in which truth "collisions" cause disagreement, misunderstanding, and breakdowns of communication. Where among your co-workers, managers, and employees are differing truths creating confusion? What's happening between family members and friends that points to multiple truths in conflict?

Worksheet

1. How do you feel about truth?

You've read the definitions and you've read how misunderstandings about truth play a part in each of the Five Deadly *Shoulds*. You've observed different situations to see what the three truths are in each one.

What observations do you have now about truth and how it operates in life and business?

(**Example**: Wow. Now I've had a chance to really observe, I can see what a very cool – and useful – concept this is. I'll admit I had a bit of trouble in the beginning – I mean, truth is truth, right? and how can there be three truths in any given situation? But I was watching Jeff and Chris discussing (um, arguing about) the schedule for the next quarter, and it just popped into my head, so loudly that I thought everyone around me should have heard it: They've got colliding truths. Jeff wants his team to have a breather – they've been putting in nights and weekends for months now. That's his truth. And Chris sees the sales projections for his team, and what having the new release would do for his sales figures. That's his truth: the chance to exceed his sales projections.

And you know what? I had the courage to ask if I could make a suggestion, and because of the trust they had in me, based on the *personal power* and *responsibility* I've been working on, they stopped and listened to me. And I was able to point out what each of them is really looking for. They were amazed – and so was my boss! He thanked me after the meeting!)

2. How is this different from how you felt before?

Notice how your views about truth have shifted, even if only a little bit. Noticing how change happens is important in recognizing how you change, and understanding how to continue to change.

(**Example**: Well, it's night and day. I never would have seen what was going on before; I just would have gotten bored with the discussion and tuned out, and probably started answering email, since I generally take my laptop to meetings. This time, I was able to participate in what feels like a very powerful and exciting way!)

3. Can you identify ways in which you can use this new understanding – that there's my truth, your truth, and how with mutual understanding and collaborative negotiation they can come together to form *our* truth – in your workplace?

(**Example**: Oh, yeah! In fact, I can see myself becoming the mediator for a lot of these types of discussions! Okay, seriously, yes, it's very clear to me how useful this can be, if I just keep on doing what I did in that meeting with Chris and Jeff.)

Exercise: Learn to See the Three Truths

A nice thing about this perspective on truth is that it brings so much that would otherwise be confusing and frustrating into crystal clarity.

Yet it can be hard to step outside of your own truth long enough to look for the other person's truth.

For instance, you might feel that understanding the other person is the same as agreeing with her.

It's not; it's simply understanding. It is, of course, a reality that understanding leads to compassion and compromise – but that's just a natural unfolding, not a betrayal of your cause. You're not changing your mind; you're broadening your viewpoint.

And you won't suddenly become a negotiating wimp! In fact, the exact opposite is more likely: because you'll learn to get out of your own way and see the other person's truth and how your truth and theirs can be combined, you'll become masterful at creating real win-win results.

Exercise

In the heat of the moment and when you're not used to this way of thinking, it's difficult to step away from the emotional demands of your own truth to see what's going on for other people. Start out, therefore, by looking at past events to see if you can identify the truths involved in each situation.

You can do this exercise with paper and pen (which I always recommend), or on the computer if you'd rather. In either event, schedule about an hour and a half to two hours to complete the exercise. Plan to go back and review what you write over the next few days and weeks to see what new insights pop up for you.

Start by thinking back over the last few days, weeks, or months. Work backwards; pick events that happened recently if you can, rather than in the distant past. Your memories and perceptions will be more clear.

Think of three different instances of conflict or discussion, situations in which there was some sort of disagreement between two people. At least two of these should involve you; the third can involve you or be an instance where you were observing other people. At least two should be work-related; the third can be work-related or personal. (If you do include one instance where you were observing, it's best if that is one of your work-related scenarios.)

Start by writing a very brief, one- or two-sentence description of what happened in each case, each one on its own sheet of paper. For instance, "In a meeting about the project schedule, I disagreed with Dan about the best approach for getting sign-off from the stakeholders on Phase I." Then write down the outcome for each. "Dan was so stubborn that I finally just gave up, but I still disagree with him and I'll probably approach the stakeholders my way anyway."

You now have three pages, each with a brief situation description and outcome at the top. You'll complete each one in turn, according to the steps outlined here.

Next, think about what your truth was in the situation. Write down, in detail, what you knew to be real and what your reasons were for the position you took.

Now, pause for a moment. In writing your position, your truth, you've put yourself back into the situation and you're probably feeling some of the same emotions you felt at the time, even if not quite as intensely. Perhaps you're angry, frustrated, nervous, impatient.

Write down, without stopping to think, all the emotions you feel/felt. It's these emotions that get in your way, that keep you from even *seeing*, never mind acting upon, the other person's truth.

Note, please, that I'm not saying you're wrong for feeling the emotions. Emotions *are*; they can't be wrong or right. Nor should you try to stop feeling them (as if you could).

Instead, create a little breathing space for yourself by acknowledging how you feel instead of just using those un-named feelings to fuel your argument or trying to stuff them away because you think you "shouldn't" feel them. Then you can then look past all that and get a glimpse of the other person's truth.

Do that now: write down what you think the other person's truth was in this situation.

When you believe you've described it fully, think for a moment and go deeper. Write at least another two or three sentences; there's always more to draw out, especially when you're new at this.

Next, identify where the two truths were colliding. What were the key disconnects that created disagreement between you and the other person?

Finally, explore the potential for shared truth. What might have been more satisfying and created more productive outcomes?

Complete these steps for all three of your scenarios, and you'll be well on your way to being ready to do this in the moment as situations arise. Just remember to start by identifying and acknowledging the emotions you're feeling. You can do this quickly with a deep breath and an internal question: "What am I feeling?" Then see through those emotions to perceive the other person's truth and discover where the shared truth lies.

Courage

Does courage sound to you – as it did to the Cowardly Lion in L. Frank Baum's The Wizard of Oz – like something that everyone *except* you has? I'm going to en*courage* you to think differently!

Mary Anne Radmacher, American writer and artist, wrote, "Courage doesn't always roar. Sometimes courage is the little voice at the end of the day that says... I'll try again tomorrow."

A New Definition

The Fifth Dragon, "Senior management should know what they're doing at all times," introduced the idea that courage is not just about standing up and speaking out; it's about doing so with care for your own protection at the same time.

COURAGE

It takes courage to put your ideas forward to people who are senior to you, and it really takes courage to stand up and speak out when something's going wrong or your opinion might be unpopular with your co-workers, employees, or management.

Fortunately, there are ways to make it easier on yourself as well as to protect yourself from the potential fallout.

Like the Cowardly Lion, you might feel you need something you don't have in order to be courageous.

You might feel you need more money in the bank, or a deeply committed romantic relationship, or more education, or children.

If you had these things, you would have something worth being courageous about.

Or you might feel like you need to be unafraid to have courage. And that, of course, couldn't be farther from reality.

In fact, especially if you've been working through the previous exercises, you already have everything you need.

You have your own integrity: your desire to be successful *and* stay within your integrity, living by your values.

You now know what it's like to stand in your personal power and act from that strong foundation.

You know the transformative feeling of taking responsibility for *all* the outcomes of your actions, not just your mistakes.

You know how to prove your trustworthiness to others, based on your power, responsibility, and integrity.

And you know how to understand the other person's truth, and how colliding truths create miscommunication and disagreement.

Remember that courage, as Radmacher says, is about knowing which battles to fight and which to leave alone. As Kim learned in the case study on trust, courage mis-applied can get you in trouble without creating anything close to the outcome you desired.

And as the Cowardly Lion learned, courage exists within us all; it's just a question of finding what matters and having the right foundation under your feet.

In Action

What examples of courage-in-action can you find in your day? Where is there the quiet courage that people show when they walk away from a battle, or when they take a moment to help someone even though their day is already over-full, or when they put forward an idea in a group that might be unwilling or unready to hear it?

Where can you see examples of when courage wasn't wielded, when someone abdicated their power and chose to keep silent?

Worksheet

1. How do you feel about courage?

You've read the definitions and you've read how courage – misplaced or a lack thereof – helps you fight each of the Five Deadly *Shoulds*. You've looked for examples of courage in the actions of managers, co-workers, employees, as well as with your family and friends.

What observations do you have now about courage and how it operates in life and business?

(**Example**: This is interesting. I always thought of courage as being big and flashy – you know, soldiers going into battle, astronauts getting into the space shuttle, that kind of thing. I don't think I ever thought about it from the perspective of everyday life. And now that I am, I find I'm really touched by the ways that people *do* show courage – sometimes, even though this sounds like a cliché, just by getting out of bed and facing another day.)

2. How is this different from how you felt before?

Notice how your views about courage have shifted, even if only a little bit. Noticing how change happens is important in recognizing how you change, and understanding how to continue to change.

(**Example**: I really don't think I ever considered courage before, at least, not in a personal every-day sense. And I'm finding that in observing, it's coloring my perception of many people who are doing a lot of things. For instance, my friend Susie, who just started a new job and told me that she's terrified of her boss. But she's going to work with a smile every day, and she's already making a difference.)

3. Can you identify ways in which you can recognize your own courage, and how you can make it easier for you to be courageous in difficult situations?

(**Example**: Wow. That's a tough question. But I see how this builds on the other qualities: personal power, responsibility, trust, and truth. Well, I'm going to look for ways to stand on that foundation and take risks. And I don't mean risks like speeding on the freeway. I mean risks like offering compromises in challenging situations (the three truths!), like really hearing what people say instead of drawing conclusions, like offering help when someone seems to be struggling. That feels good.)

Exercise: Practice Smart Courage

Developing a greater understanding of your courage is a process of awareness and conscious choice-making. It's not about suddenly leaping into battle or taking up big causes; it's about noticing the sometimes quite small opportunities where you truly can make a difference, and then choosing to take action. Though the idea of courage can seem very BIG and somewhat threatening, the practice of it is usually more subtle, and always powerful.

Mary Anne Radmacher's quote (above) is a terrific description of the wisdom of what I call "smart courage." Kim, from the Third Dragon's case study, learned after the fact that worthwhile battles can pull you into un-worthwhile actions; she certainly learned firsthand that "smart courage" is a skill worth cultivating.

You'll have found that your courage has been increasing as you work through these exercises. And you've undoubtedly noticed that all the qualities build on and support each other, especially Power. When you step into your personal power, you discover that courage takes on a new dimension, a new reality, a new possibility. Add in Responsibility and Trust and your understanding of the three Truths, and you have the foundation you need to begin to work with and act from Courage.

Exercise

Get out your trusty pen and good paper again, and think back over the last week. Draw a line down the middle of two pages to make two columns on each.

On the first sheet of paper, in the left-hand column, list all the times and situations when you exercised courage. Maybe you made the right suggestion, even though it was unpopular. Maybe you stopped someone from spreading hurtful gossip, perhaps just by walking away from it and choosing not to listen. Whatever it was, and operating on what's courageous for *you* (which may or may not be for someone else), add it to the list. It's all too easy to overlook our own acts of courage, so be sure to notice even what may seem like the smallest instances!

For the second list, on the second sheet of paper and in the left-hand column, look at some of the situations where you *didn't* act. Perhaps you kept silent in a difficult meeting when you had an idea that might have helped (but might not have). Maybe you saw the result of colliding truths, but you were late to an appointment and didn't say anything – and then forgot to follow up. Again, whatever your list has on it, it's *your* list, and holds only those things that are meaningful to you, not things that are according to anyone else's ideas.

Going back to your first list, in the right-hand column write quick notes about the outcomes. Did you get the results you wanted? You don't need lengthy explanations; just a quick yes/no/partly will do.

On the second list, note down what you gained *and* lost by not stepping forward. You'll find that in some cases, there was no loss at all – and you might have gained something (time, for instance). Or you might have gained time, but lost respect for yourself.

Or you might have actually *gained* respect for yourself, since you kept yourself out of a sticky situation.

Note that there are times when you thought you walked away without exercising courage, but in fact you were exercising *smart* courage by choosing your battles.

Note that there are times when you do indeed lose integrity by walking away.

Note that there are times when you don't walk away, and you lose anyway. If you had walked away, what would you have gained and lost?

This is all about understanding how smart courage doesn't always look the way you might expect. And it's about really getting to the core of what you gain or lose when you act – and don't act.

AFTERWORD

You may have noticed that many of the suggestions and stories I tell involve recommendations or strong hints that you take action to understand what's going on around you, study and learn to understand the people you work with, observe where you need to take responsibility for work well done, communicate, step into your personal power, and get more involved.

That might feel like a lot of work.

It might seem as if this is more conscious effort than you may want to exert in your job, effort that isn't, as far as you can see, directly related to the actual job you're doing – the specific tasks you need to do order to complete your work and go home at a reasonable hour. When you're wrestling with an overloaded schedule and an impossible to-do list, adding this sort of high-intensity mental and emotional work can seem impossible and unreasonable.

Just as all these Dragons, these Deadly *Shoulds*, are fallacies, so is this concept that it's too much effort to become proficient at fighting the Dragons and reclaiming your career.

Yes, there's effort involved, and like any learning process, that effort is more intense early on. As you build new patterns and habits, it becomes less so.

But much more than that, the work I suggest here has an almost miraculous way of *saving* time, and fairly quickly, too.

Why?

Because when you stop letting the Dragons control your career, you develop a powerful ability to cut to the chase, eliminate unnecessary beating around the bush, and simply *get done what needs to be done.*

And when you stop letting these Dragons control your career, you begin feeling better about yourself, more confident in your capabilities and capacity to excel and succeed, and happier with your job – all of which leads to greater success, in your career and in your life.

Isn't that worth a little effort?

ABOUT THE AUTHOR

Grace Judson is a team dynamics and communication coach and an instigator of meaningful strategic change.

For 16 years, she held executive leadership positions in global organizations, including Munich American Re and EMC Document Sciences, where she led strategic process initiatives that created significant improvements in customer satisfaction, sales success, and risk management. Realizing she could have a more meaningful impact in the world as an external strategic business consultant, she started her business in 2005.

She's dedicated to helping business owners, leaders, and teams solve tough communication and workflow problems so they realign with their purpose and make more money doing work they love – while staying true to their desire to change the world.

With a degree in writing from Bard College, Grace has trained as an executive and life coach and is a certified Realization Process teacher. A long-term volunteer with the Association for Talent Development (formerly the American

---

Society for Training & Development), Grace served on the Board of the San Diego chapter for four years, including President of the Board in 2013. She's taught business and communication courses at local colleges and university extensions, and has written six e-books, including *Office Politics: the elephant in the conference room*. She frequently leads workshops, seminars, and retreats on subjects ranging from communication and business strategy to organizational and gender politics.

Find further details about Grace and her work on her website http://www.gracejudson.com.

There, you can browse her extensive blog, covering topics of leadership, meaningful change, real communication, and strategic action.

Plus, you can sign up to receive her periodic emails, which cover blog topics, special events and offers, and notices of articles and other materials published around the Web.

PRAISE FOR THE BOOK

"I have been reading *The Five Deadly Shoulds of Office Politics* from cover to cover for the past few hours. It is fantastic and so very relevant to my life at this particular juncture.

Many thanks for sharing your insights on your Web site and in your newsletters – now I know that I am not crazy. Your perspective has helped me see that I fall into the category of being unwilling to compromise my integrity and 'play the game." I know I have always been willing (and preferred) to deal with the negative consequences that result from that decision rather than drink the Kool-Aid.

Reading *The Five Deadly Shoulds* has helped me understand the third option that I had never considered, and has provided me an opportunity for another turning point. I am already a leader, I bring a unique skillset, AND I have a LOT of experience with TERRIBLE supervisors – so surely I can do better!

Your book has helped me see that I don't have to drink the Kool-Aid, and that I have a responsibility to use what I know to help others succeed. If I don't, then I will be letting myself down and and hurting myself simply because I am unwilling to move outside of my comfort zone. "

– June Louise Simon, Atlanta, Georgia

"I recently gave a speech to my Toastmaster's group. My speech was a reflection of your book *The Five Deadly Shoulds of Office Politics*, which is outstanding. Thanks so...o...o much. I love it. You have hit on issues that many coaches and mentors just ignore."

– Gwendolyn Washington, U.S. Department of Education

Praise for Grace

"Six months ago, I would have said corporate politics is who you have to back-stab to get ahead. When Grace told me that, as a manager, I had to learn to understand politics, I almost changed my mind about working with her. *Politics* was a four-letter word in my mind.

It didn't take long her her to teach me that politics is really about working within the process to do what needs to be done – working with my peers, my team, and my management to move the company forward without stepping on anyone else's toes. It's about how to form a team and be a leader even when the company's leadership isn't making the effort. More importantly, it's how to do all that while *caring* for the success of everyone.

I know I'm a better, more confident manager, and I'm getting more done by working within our company processes more effectively. My boss trusts me not to screw up politically any more. In fact, she even commented on my improvement in my last performance review!

– Paul Jones, Resources Development Manager, San Diego, California

"People don't realize that you don't tell me what to do, you just help me think through what I was already thinking. I don't think people realize that's what it's all about. They don't know whether your opinion is something that they want to be influenced by, but that's not what you're doing.

You've always helped me figure out what it is that *I'm* thinking, without saying, "Here's what I think you should do." You help me find a different perspective that validates and makes me think differently about the decisions I'm trying to make.

You told me that a lot of people tend to make their decisions based on what other people are thinking. That was really a *huge* part of what was causing me to not be sure about what I wanted to do, but I didn't realize that was why. I never would have said, "Oh I'm so worried about what so-and-so thinks." I didn't think I was, but I was!

Every time I've talked to you, I've been pleased with the way you make me think about things and also just the knowledge you have about *everything* – seriously!"

– Lisa O'Reilly, Senior Vice President, Professional Services North America, Escondido, California

"In the year plus that we worked together, there were a lot of changes that I was going through. Having the coaching helped me stay grounded through that transition and change. The only way anyone is going to change behavior is by identifying the problem, reviewing it with a coach, getting the feedback, working at it, looking at it again – it's an ongoing process. It's not a one-time thing. How else are you going to get this information? How else are you going to develop?

Having that objective person who will help you look at your life and situation in objective terms is worth the price of admission!"

– Lauren Midgley, MBA, business consultant and coach, Colleyville, Texas

"You created an environment for us to think together and recognize what we want.

You listened carefully to our different perspectives, some overlapping, some complimentary, some differentiated. You were able to receive whatever deeper expressions needed to be there without getting lost in philosophy. And you were able to feed it all back, to reflect, integrate, and clarify, synthesize and remove emotionality, and show us how things I might have thought were in conflict were actually complementary.

It was like you had a mandala in your head. It wasn't a pre-ordained template, but instead you were responding to what we were bringing up. So you filled it in according to what we had to say, and then you could point out what was missing and ask what's the next step.

There was humor, a sense of lightness, a lot of practicality. There was ease. You didn't ease off, you leaned in, but there was an ease and a consistency.

Devi and I are very comfortable as facilitators, but leadership is different. Leadership is owning and embodying the call, disturbing the dream, disturbing the space, being more provocative by declaring things. You helped me become more comfortable and more clear about my leadership role.

– Eric Klein, executive coach, author, and meditation instructor, Encinitas, California

"Grace has brought a much needed wisdom, and the skills to allow us to apply that wisdom, into our organization. Her understanding of the challenges of having a well rounded and fulfilling life (ie, having your cake and eating it, too) make her coaching relevant for most of us. She blends her vast corporate knowledge and experience (including high level technological and systems development) with her outside the box thinking, creating results that are immediately applicable while creating pathways for a new approach to whatever you are doing. I truly enjoy working with Grace, as she is not afraid to disagree nor is she afraid to laugh. Both are qualities I find refreshing and critical to any change process.

– Shannon Thompson, nonprofit Executive Director, San Diego, California